William C. Morgan

Shoes and Shoemaking Illustrated

A Brief Sketch of the History and Manufacture of Shoes from the Earliest Time

William C. Morgan

Shoes and Shoemaking Illustrated

A Brief Sketch of the History and Manufacture of Shoes from the Earliest Time

ISBN/EAN: 9783743402645

Manufactured in Europe, USA, Canada, Australia, Japa

Cover: Foto ©ninafisch / pixelio.de

Manufactured and distributed by brebook publishing software (www.brebook.com)

William C. Morgan

Shoes and Shoemaking Illustrated

ADVERTISEMENTS

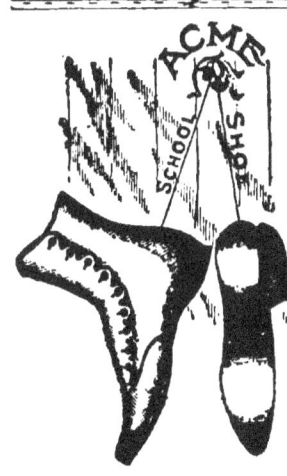

F. A. Seavey & Co.,
Manufacturers of
Ladies', Misses' and Children's FINE SHOES, in Button, Lace and Oxfords.

F. A. Seavey & Co.,
BEVERLY, - - MASS.
Boston Office, 1 Lincoln Street.

If You Want
anything in Drug Store Goods

Get it AT GREEN'S
HE CUTS THE PRICE.

and you will save from **25 to 33** per cent.

Prompt and Courteous Attention by reliable men, whether your wants are small or large.

Green the Druggist, Beverly, Mass.

ADVERTISEMENTS

A Tip on Tips.

Every one is looking for tips, some one kind, and some another. We deal in the **PATENT LEATHER** kind. If you are in need of any—Try us.

Leslie A. Merrill,

83 Rantoul St., Beverly, Mass.

Don't Read This

Unless you wish to learn something of value to you.

The Ideal Benefit Association is "Ideal" because

1st. It has in its plan eliminated the weak points in other organizations, included their strong points, and added others.
2nd It pays for sickness, injuries, and death.
3rd. It includes both sexes.
4th. It pays for sixteen weeks' sickness in any year.
5th. It permits $25 a week with only $100 on life.
6th. It allows you to take 5, 10, 15, 20 or $25 a week.
7th. It allows you to take $100 to $3000 at death.

The membership fee is from $2 to $12, according to the amount desired.

Drop the Association a card with your address, and an agent will call upon you.

122 CABOT ST., - BEVERLY, MASS.

ADVERTISEMENTS

Joseph W. Obear,

Turning, Scroll Sawing, and fine Pattern Work.

All Orders promptly attended to.

Cor. Park and West Dane St.,   –   Beverly, Mass

F. W. BERNARD, Beverly, Mass.
Artistic Memorials in Granite, Marble & Bronze.

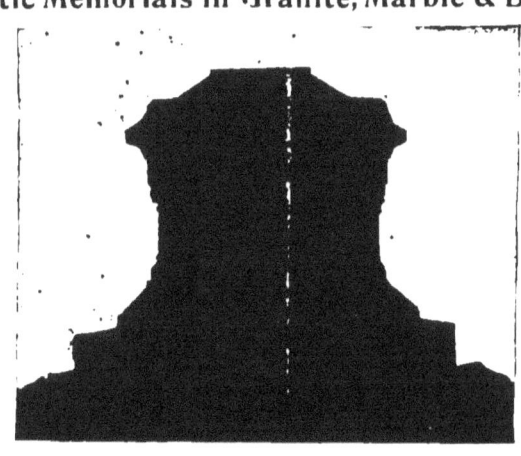

Correspondence solicited.

Special Designs furnished Free of charge.

ADVERTISEMENTS

E. F. SULLIVAN,

Agent for the

Hanover Bicycle

For Cash or on Time,

Also agent for the

CELEBRATED

Jacob Doll Piano

Cash or on Time.

7 Washington St.,

BEVERLY.

ADVERTISEMENTS

FACTS.

People now realize the fact that it is cheaper to own a house than to pay rent.

Many are moving to the northern section of the city to get away from the east winds which are injurious to the throat and lungs.

If you are thinking of making a purchase or moving, now is the time to secure a cosy home at a very low cost and very easy terms in one of the prettiest spots in the City on the western slope of Prospect Hill, nice level lots from 4500 to 7000 feet each.

New seven room cottages, all modern conveniences, substantially built, open for inspection to anyone. Equal to any custom build house. Three already sold, will build on any of the remaining forty-five lots to suit.

Also some fine house lots for sale very reasonable.

These being the only available lots in City proper at a reasonable price it will be for your interest to investigate before purchasing. Prices are sure to please. Fifty or more references. Inquire of

PRINCE OBER,
OFFICE: 363 Cabot St., Beverly.

CLAFLIN BROS.,
PLUMBING,
Machine Jobbing of All Kinds.
Steam, Gas and Water Piping.

All Orders Promptly Attended To.

60 RAILROAD AVE., BEVERLY, MASS.

J. H. CLAFLIN, Practical Plumber.

John H. Claflin.   Edward E. Claflin.

ADVERTISEMENTS

SMITH & McLARREN, Park St., Beverly, Mass.

Stair Builders.

Brackets, Rails, Newels, Posts and Balusters.

Planing and Sawing of all kinds.

Estimates given on All Kinds of Stair Work.

Dr. E. B. DUDLEY,

DENTIST,

107 Cabot Street,

BEVERLY, - MASS.

ADVERTISEMENTS

M. GRADY,

Stone Mason & Contractor.

Estimates Given on all kinds of Stone Work.

Elliot Street, = Beverly, Mass.

Woodbury Electric Co.,

Wiring of Every Description at Short Notice.

Isolated Electric Plants Installed.

Chandeliers, Cluster Lights, Globes.

Gas Lighting a Specialty.

General Electric Work of all Kinds.

Bell Work, Speaking Tubes, Etc.

J. W. LEE, Manager,
Cor. Dane and Lothrop Sts., Beverly, Mass.

ADVERTISEMENTS
FOR INSURANCE

GO TO

MURNEY,

ROOM 8,

Endicott Building, - Beverly.

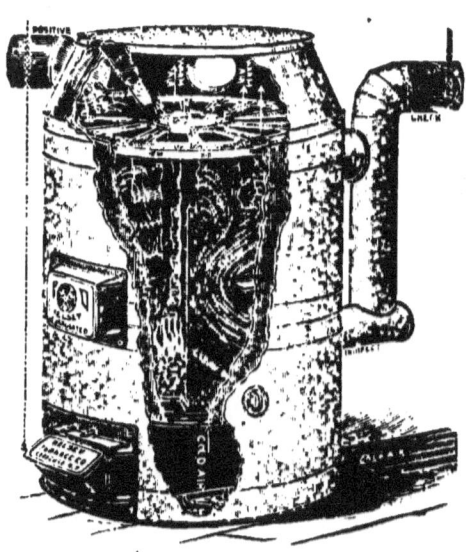

Any one wishing to purchase a HEATER would do well to call and see the KELSEY HEATER, also a fine line of Ranges Oil and Gasoline Stoves.

C. L. WOODBURY,
277 CABOT ST.

ADVERTISEMENTS

Beverly News Company,

Agents for all

Boston Daily, Weekly and

Sunday Newspapers.

Also for all the Leading Magazines and Local Newspapers.

Choice Line of
Confectionery and Cigars.

What Does I. T. WEBBER Keep?

Rather, what does he not have—Cloth from a Kentucky Jean at 35 cents, to the Finest Broadcloth.

All Wool Pants that will fit boys from 3 to 12 yrs.

At the present time, a big drive in Men's and Youths' Pants, all wool, at $2.00. Size 29 to 50 waist.

A full line of Braids, Buttons, and Trimmings for repairing.

A good cutter, good journeymen tailors, and low prices for first-class custom tailoring.

ISRAEL T. WEBBER.
Atlantic Block.

ADVERTISEMENTS

TAKING CHANCES

is all very well in some cases. Not in buying articles for your table. If there's a place where you know you'll get reliable goods at fair prices, that's the place to go. Risk is too great to chance going to another place. Save time by coming at once to

Bell's Market and Grocery.

Beverly Repair Shop & Supply Store,
F. A. E. HAMILTON, Prop. and Manager.

To Everybody—We carry a full line of Hardware.

To Farmers—If you want Agricultural Tools or Seeds this is the place to buy them.

To Shoemakers—Just remember that you can procure any and all shoe tools and instruments at

HAMILTON'S
Cor. Pond and Rantoul Sts.,   Beverly, Mass.

Bicycle and Lawn Mowers a Specialty.

ADVERTISEMENTS

Janson's Studio,
156 CABOT STREET.

Photographs finished in Carbon, Carbonette or Ivory.

Crayons, Pastels and Water Colors a Specialty.

Have you seen our $5.00 16x20 Water Colors? They are fine, call and judge for yourself.

WE GIVE SATISFACTION.

Carbonettes and Ivory Finish Photographs a specialty.

First-class Work Guaranteed.

Children's Photographs taken by the Instantaneous Process.

Pictures are warranted not to fade.

F. L. Hildreth, Photographer,
140 CABOT STREET, CITY.

ADVERTISEMENTS

Ladies

To Learn

Dressmaking

Position When Learned,

$10 to $15 Weekly.

First-class Dressmaking.

Satisfaction Guaranteed.

OPENED 9 A. M. TO 9 P. M.

✸✸✸✸✸✸

M. E. Sullivan,

168 Cabot Street,

BEVERLY,   =   MASS.

ADVERTISEMENTS

Busiest House in the City.

Webb, the Jeweler

- Dealer in -

Watches, Clocks, Jewelry, Silverware, Silver Novelties, Optical Goods, etc.

Repairing a Specialty.

Satisfaction Guaranteed.

Masonic Building, Beverly, Mass.

O. B. Burnham,

Dealer in Meal, Corn, Oats, Fine Feed, Shorts, Etc. Loose and Baled Hay and Straw.

187 and 189 Rantoul Street,

BEVERLY, - . MASS.

CONNECTED BY TELEPHONE.

ADVERTISEMENTS

Carriages.

Rubber Tires For Carriages.
You must have them for Comfort.
You must have them for Pleasure.
You want them for General Use.
   We are putting them on at Wholesale Prices.

E. C. SAWYER,
126 Rantoul St., Cor. Bow St., Beverly.

We have first-class goods, good service, quick delivery, trade is increasing. Please send in your orders early.

Remember, We give 16 oz. to the pound, and 8 qts. to the peck.

We have two Stores,
   231 and 233 Cabot Street,
   208 Rantoul Street.

A. F. Place.

ADVERTISEMENTS

To the Ladies of Beverly.

We wish to call your attention to the fact that we have taken the agency for the celebrated Bazaar Glove Fitting Patterns, of which we have a large stock constantly on hand, at the very low price of **15 cents a Pattern,** irrespective of marked prices. Call and examine counter book. Monthly Fashion Guides Fr ee.

Dealers in Dry and Fancy Goods, Hosiery, Ginghams, Dress Linings, etc. Wrappers a Specialty. Prices always the Lowest.

The Bazaar Pattern Store,
   265 Cabot Street, Beverly.

Beverly Pool Rooms,
7 RAILROAD AVENUE,

is the place to play Pool, and buy your Cigars.

Catering for Parties. Fish Dinners a specialty.

H. P. JOHNSON & CO.
PROPRIETORS.

ADVERTISEMENTS

WE ARE HEADQUARTERS

For

Bicycle,

Tennis

and Sporting Shoes.

E. Putnam, The Shoeman,

Odd Fellows' Block, Beverly.

CATERING.

All Tastes satisfied, from the epicurean down to the humblest workman.

After years of experience, Gordon the Caterer, is still prepared to furnish Banquets, Suppers, Private Dinners, Wedding Breakfasts, etc.

Ice Cream, all flavors.

Prompt Attention. **Service Unexcelled.**

Emerson G. Gordon,
Selby House Block,
94 Cabot St., *Beverly, Mass.*

ADVERTISEMENTS

Neal & Newhall,

Beverly's

LEADING OUTFITTERS.

❦❦❦

Sole Agents For

LAMSOM & HUBBARD'S HAT.

F. D. FRASER, Manager.

Prices as low as any in the city for first-class work.

S. F. OBER & SON,

Plans and Estimates *Contractors and Builders.*
Cheerfully Furnished. Jobbing promptly attended to.
32 and 34 CENTRAL STREET.
Also, Dealers in Real Estate.

SHOES AND SHOEMAKING

ILLUSTRATED.

A Brief Sketch of the History and Manufacture of Shoes from the Earliest Time

—BY—

W. C. MORGAN.

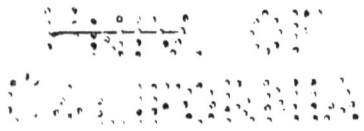

BEVERLY, MASS.:
PRESS OF KEHEW & ODELL.
1897.

TS 1000
M 6

INTRODUCTION.

In the history of Beverly, shoes and shoemaking have always been identified with her success, and many of her most prominent men have been connected with the craft. The people of this generation have watched with ever increasing interest, the development of the shoe factory right here in our midst, from the little shop in the door yard of almost every inhabitant to the large and well equipped modern factory of the present time. With the growth of the shoe industry there has also been a corresponding growth of city and property, and today we point with pride to the large and well regulated shoe factories in the manufacturing district. Incident to and connected with the shoe industry are other industries such as the manufacture of boxes and cartons, and the manufacture of shoe machinery. These factories we have here today. Beverly shoes are known throughout the country, and several Beverly boys are selling her product. It seems to the compiler of this work that a book of this kind treating of the history of shoemaking in general, and in Beverly in particular is a desirable one and one that will meet the approval and recognition of every Beverlyite no matter wherever he may be. The author is indebted to the late Hon. John I. Baker for much valuable information, to Albert Vittum and the Boot and Shoe Recorder for the use of cuts and to any and all who have furnished data or statistics.

WILLIAM C. MORGAN.

M134664

THE FIRST SHOE SHOP IN NEW ENGLAND.

CHAPTER I.

The word shoe is derived from the Anglo Saxon scoh, the general meaning of which is, any covering for the foot, excepting, of course, hosiery. This subject of shoes and shoemaking should be of great interest to our townspeople, for what Beverly is at the present time, her success and her position among her sister cities is due in no small measure to her shoe industry, that industry which has increased her population, added to her wealth, and made her the thriving city of today.

The subject is a broad one embracing, as it does, all countries and nations, as shoes of some kind are almost invariably worn except by some savage tribes. One of the first times the word shoe occurs in the Bible, if not the first time it is mentioned, is where God meets Moses on Mount Sinai and speaks to him as follows: "Take thy shoes from off thy feet for the place wheron thou standest is holy ground." These shoes were probably sandals which were the only kind then worn. We find in profane history, and we gather from the reports of scholars and travelers who have made ancient lands a study, that these sandals were worn even before this time, for from pictures reproduced and handed down to us by these explorers, and which once decorated the walls of the cities of ancient Egypt, we find that the shoemaker, or rather the sandal maker, as he must have been called occupied a prominent place among the Egyptians. One picture in particular which is supposed from the characters portrayed, as well as the articles of wearing apparel, to have decorated the walls of Thebes during the reign of Thotmes Third or about the time of the exodus of the Children of Israel from Egypt represents the shoemaker at his work.

The men, for there are two of them, are seated on low stools, one of them making holes in the thong of the sandal through which the strap passed which bound the sandal to the feet, the other sewing the thong and tightening the work with his teeth. Rather a primitive way this seems to us, in these days of the McKay, the Goodyear and Eppler & Adams machines.

The tools bear some resemblance to those used today in hand work, particularly the awl which has

SHOES AND SHOEMAKING ILLUSTRATED.

changed but little. These sandals which as we have said before were the first kind of shoe of which we find any record, were made low and fastened across the instep with leathern thongs. Those worn by the common people of Egypt were made wholly of leather, while those worn by the priests and nobility were made of palm leaves and papyrus. Wilkinson in his treatise on the manners and customs of the ancient Egyptians says, "Ladies and men of high rank paid great attention to the beauty of their sandals, but those of the middle class who were able to wear sandals, for they were considered a luxury, sometimes and on some occasions, preferred going barefoot and in religious ceremonies the priests sometimes took them off."

These sandals were of great variety in form as well as material, some of them being pointed and turning up at the toes like our old fashioned skates. The Persians during the reign of Darius and Xerxes wore many kinds of shoes. Hall tells us that there were three prominent varieties, the half sandal, the shoe, and the boot or high shoe. Among the ancient Greeks and Romans there were few who wore shoes, these few being members of the royal family, senators, and nobles. The senators in particular were

SHOES AND SHOEMAKING ILLUSTRATED.

very dressy in the matter of their shoes, some of which were black, with a crescent of gold or silver on the instep, while others were decorated with ornamental work in painting or embroidery, and some were even studded with jewels.

There were two kinds of shoes in vogue at this time, the Solea, which we have described above, and the Calceus, which were made like wooden shoes and which were designed more particularly for out of door wear. Hope tells us that the Grecian ladies wore shoes laced in front and lined with the furs of animals of the cat tribe, whose heads and claws adorned the top, and dangled down over the instep, quite a fancy ankle decoration certainly.

The Egyptian shoe was woven of strong river grass and other vegetable material, but was very rarely made of leather, the priests of Egypt believing that the person was defiled by contact with anything that had been killed.

According to Homer the Greeks wore boots to battle in the time of Agamemnon. Plato strongly opposed the wearing of shoes. On entering the house the shoes were removed as is the custom in the east today.

Among the peasants of France, Holland, Belgium

SHOES AND SHOEMAKING ILLUSTRATED.

and Germany, heavy wooden shoes called "sabots" are worn as has been the custom for centuries. These sabots are mostly made in Brittany in the northern part of France. An ax, saw, drill, gouge, and plane are all the tools required in the manufacture of these heavy wooden shoes. The work is done in the forests and whole families are engaged in it.

Sherwood in an article in Frank Leslie's some years ago since says, "Shoes have played an important part in the romances of all ages. In our earliest childhood we delighted in the adventures of Cinderella; or the little glass slipper." This story is older than the very language in which our nurses told it, and it comes down to us accompanied by a sort of moldering and exquisite perfume from amidst the papyrus archives which modern science has learned to translate from Egyptian Hieroglyphics. Pti a beautiful Persian princess was taken captive by an Egyptian general, who brought her with the rest of his spoils, to his home on the banks of the Nile. One day after bathing her lovely self in the waters of the great river, and before she had finished her toilet, Pti was startled by the vision of a youth as beautiful as the Sun God, who ran toward her from a neighboring thicket.

SHOES AND SHOEMAKING ILLUSTRATED.

"The youth would have caught her in his arms, but the lovely Pti was a true daughter of Dian, and being swift of foot, escaped his embrace leaving in her flight a tiny glass slipper. This the youth treasured and through its medium was enabled to discover its lovely owner. The Persians alone manufactured glass shoes in those days; the lovely woman was therefore a Persian. The general had brought a train of captives with him from the land of flowers and glass slippers. How easy the following of such a clue when Cupid placed the first link of evidence, the crystal slipper in the youth's hand. And the youth was none other than a prince of blood royal, Ramesis II, the original of the great statue of Memnon, the singing statute, which stands on the bank of the river Nile today. When Pti was at last found she fled no more from her princely lover; but as his wife lived long and happy, and her cartouche is placed beside his in the greatest of all the pyramids."

Writers and poets of all ages have used the theme of a woman's shoe from the time of Horace who describes a coquettish Roman beauty tightening the straps of her sandals around her pretty ankles, down to that of T. B. Aldrich in whose "Queen of Sheba" the little slipper of the heroine plays so important a part in the life and character of the hero. It is said that of all races Americans have the most beautiful feet. Several familiar proverbs relate to shoes. "Waiting for dead men's shoes." "I would not stand in his shoes." "Too big for his shoes." "I prefer to be trodden on by the velvet slipper rather than the wooden shoe" are some of the expressions.

High shoes reaching nearly to the middle of the leg were worn by men of high rank in the Tenth century. The Normans wore shoes very simple in form and made of leather. The early kings of England are represented as wearing shoes decorated with bands of silver and gold representing leather. During the Fourteenth century, shoes were made of a peculiar style some of them nearly two feet long and tapering to a point; these were brought up and tied at the knee. Some very fashionable young men wore them of different colors, for instance; one boot of red, the other of a yellow colored leather. From this style fashion suddenly changed, for fashion like fortune is fickle, from one extreme to the other,

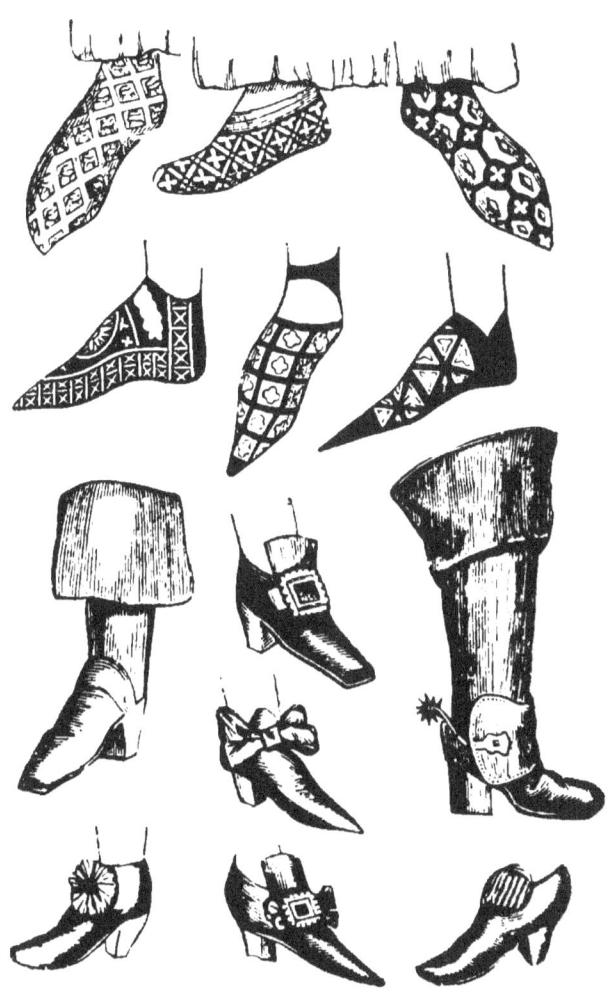

A GROUP OF OLD STYLE SHOES.

SHOES AND SHOEMAKING ILLUSTRATED.

and shoes were worn which were nearly as broad as they were long. In fact the fashion was carried to such an extent that Queen Mary was obliged to prohibit the wearing of shoes which were more than six inches broad.

High heels are of no recent origin, but on the contrary are very old for as early as the beginning of the Seventeenth century we find, from representations of costumes of that time, that the heels of shoes were worn very high, some of them being three or four inches high, so that the French heel of recent years, instead of being a new invention, is but an old and injurious fashion restored, and enough cannot be said against them, for they are not only injurious but also unhealthy.

The present form of the shoe was adopted in the Seventeenth century, and in the latter part of the same century shoe buckles were used and these continued to be used until the beginning of the present century. The most curious of all shoes are those worn by the Chinese women in high stations. They are very small some of them being not over three or four inches in length. When very young the Chinese girls have their feet bound so tight with bandages that growth is stopped which of course is very painful, but what of that as long as it is fashionable, and there is really no foot at all, only a little sort of a bunch or ball of flesh, bearing no resemblance to a foot except that the shape of the toes are visible. In Japan sandals of straw are worn. In South America sandals made of plaited thongs of hemp are used to cover the foot and we are all more or less familiar with the moccasin of the North American Indian.

SHOP IN WHICH WOODBURY BROS. COMMENCED BUSINESS.

CHAPTER II.

Adam Smith, in a work published some time since said "The excessive consumption of leather indicates a superior degree of civilization. America today is one of the greatest consumers of leather in its varied forms of manufacture, and it is universally acknowledged that the civilization of the United States is of the highest grade." We are all of us more or less familiar with the little shoemaker's shop which formerly occupied a corner in the yard of every farmer, and which during the winter was made a source of profit to himself and family by the manufacture of shoes. There was no noise of machinery, for the work was all done by hand and the outfit was a small one but these little shops were busy places.

The well to do people of those times as well as others perhaps not so well to do, but who did'nt have much of an inclination to work, and their descendants are with us today, would gather there and with the shoemaker discuss the questions of the day. In these little 12 x 16 shops many theological and politi-

SHOES AND SHOEMAKING ILLUSTRATED.

cal questions were settled, for the shoemakers of the olden time as well as the the followers of the craft today were as well read and instructed as any class of our citizens.

We remember even those of us who are still young, the little low bench with the seat on one end and the place for the "kit" on the other, and that kit also. Two or three knives, lapstone, hammer, strap, shave, long stick, shoulder stick, awls, bristles and thread in the small drawers in the lower part of the bench, also the tub of water in the middle of the floor containing the sticks or balls of wax. These are all familiar to many of us and now today as we look at our large factories filled with the most delicate yet simple machinery, capable of performing the work of many men, we can see what immense strides this industry has made during the century.

The manufacture of boots and shoes is now acknowledged as one of the principal and most important industries in the United States. As long ago as 1858 Richardson says in a work published in London, "The Americans are rapidly securing to themselves a superiority over all other nations in this important industry and in a few years all shoes of American manufacture will be regarded as the Ne Plus Ultra of the

SHOES AND SHOEMAKING ILLUSTRATED.

art." We find that shoes were made in many private families for home use, among the early settlers while those for Sunday wear and dress up occasions were imported from the mother country.

Although shoes were made in many Masachusetts towns, yet the centre of the business seems to have been from the early history of the trade, in Lynn. For we read in an old work describing this business, that the town of Lynn from its earliest settlement was noted for its shoemaking which was one of its chief industries, and it was with such facilities that shoes were made there, that it led to the saying that shoes grew spontaneously in Lynn. If these things could be said many years ago what can we say today with our shops filled with machinery and every modern labor saving device which are so plentiful in every well regulated shoe factory. The work was done in the families of the manufacturers in the early history of the business, there being no factories the business was necessarily conducted on a small scale. In 1750 however, a new start was given to the business by one John Adam Dagyr, a Welsh shoemaker who at that time had just settled in Lynn. This man by his superior workmanship and his fidelity to business, achieved for himself no mean reputa-

WOODBURY BROS. 2nd SHOP.

SHOES AND SHOEMAKING ILLUSTRATED.

tion and greatly improved the then existing styles of work. The Continental army during the Revolution was supplied with shoes made in Massachusetts.

After the close of the war, and our ports had been opened to foreign vessels, shoes began to be imported as our people were in no condition at that time to compete with European manufacturers. It was not long, however, that shoe business was dull, as the saying is today, for in 1788, the city of Lynn exported 100,000 pairs of shoes; and in 1795, 300,000 pairs were manufactured and there were employed in that city, 200 master workmen and nearly 600 apprentices and journeymen. The first vessel to carry a full cargo of boots and shoes sailed for New York during May, 1818, Shipments had been made for sometime previous, but this was the first vessel that had ever carried boots and shoes exclusively. At that time the manufacture was confined almost wholly to New England, but it soon spread and increased until in 1829 there were four jobbing boot and shoe houses in New York and Boston; during the same year the wholesale dealers handled about 1,000,000 pairs. The trade kept gradually increasing in the United States until in 1858, there were 218 wholesale and jobbing boot and shoe houses, and through these houses passed the number

SHOES AND SHOEMAKING ILLUSTRATED.

of pairs manufactured during the year, viz: 52,000,000. One of the greatest strides made in this industry was in 1851, when the pegging machine was invented by A. C. Gallagher and which was much improved later by E. Townsend and B. F. Sturtevant of Boston. It is estimated that at the present time there are more than 2,000 of these machines in use. As two or more rows of pegs can be driven at the same time with these machines, it will be seen at a glance what a vast saving of labor is made over the old method of working with pegging awl and hammer. Another invention of equal importance which, although came later may be mentioned in connection with the former, was the McKay sewing machine, the invention of one Blake and still called in England the Blake perfected by Gordon McKay and which proved to be a great bonanza to the patentee and owners.

From the following statistics, we can see the steady increase of the business from 1845 to 1880. We are aware that statistics are dry reading and are very often shunned and slighted by the average reader, but we think this subject of great importance to the people of Beverly, for from this business a large portion of our community derive their income and support. We shall confine ourselves in these figures to

SHOES AND SHOEMAKING ILLUSTRATED.

our own state, for Massachusetts is the banner state in this industry and it will be of much more interest to us than would general statistics. In 1845 the value of boots and shoes manufactured was $14,799,140; number of pairs made, 20,896,372; number of persons engaged in the work, 45,877. In 1845—value, $37,501,725; number of pairs made, 45,066,828; persons engaged in the work, 77,827. In 1857 in the city of Lynn, there were about 5,000 workmen and nearly 4,000,000 pairs manufactured. In the town of Milford during the same year there were manufactured 2,000,000 pairs. In 1865—value $56,113,987; number of pairs, 31,070,581; persons employed, 52,821. We see by comparing the figures of 1855 and 1865, that less shoes were made and the value much increased. This is of course easily explained by the fact that during the war, less work was done, because there were fewer men at home to do it, but what shoes were made commanded the highest prices. In 1875, the value of the goods manufactured was $89,375,792; number of persons employed, 49,708. The number of working hours through the state averages ten hours per day. The wages paid during the year ending May 1st, 1875, averaged $525 for each male, and $300 for each female employed. The total amount paid out in the state during the same period was $18,727,124; of which $3,687,077 was paid in Lynn or nearly 20 per cent. of the amount of capital invested, $18,692,864. One more comparison. From the differences between the number employed in 1845 and 1875, and the difference in the value and amount of production, we see what an immense saving of labor the introduction of machinery has been, for nearly three times as many shoes were made in 1875 than in 1845, and only 3,000 more persons were engaged in the work. The entire boot and shoe production of our state is now over $100,000,000 annually. From the Massachusetts statistics of labor for 1895, we glean the following: Number of persons employed 35,741; wages paid $12,302,058; value of stock $47,888,675; value of product $76,882,713.

CHAPTER III.

This chapter is a short history of the manufacture of shoes in Beverly from its earliest settlement up to the present time, with the names of many prominent citizens who have been from time to time engaged in the work. The subject treated fully would occupy more space than we have at the present at our disposal, in fact would fill a volume; so we have gone over the field carefully, gleaning such statistics and items of information as may be most instructive and interesting to us today.

It was the custom in the early history of our country for journeymen shoemakers or "tramping jours" as they were called to travel from house to house repairing shoes, and not unfrequently they took orders for shoes to measure. These shoemakers or cordwinders and cordwainers as they were called in those days, boarded with the men for whom they were working, staying at a house until all necessary repairs in their line had been made, then going on to the next place

WOODBURY BROS. FACTORY DESTROYED BY FIRE.

and so on. In the winter they travelled on snowshoes. The earliest cordwainer of whom we have any knowledge in our city, was Andrew Elliott, who lived near the present residence of the late Israel Elliott, a descendent, on Cabot Street, just above Beckford St. This part of the town was called "Haymarket" also "The City" and was a very important place and a center of trade.

Mr. Elliott was the first town clerk of Beverly and from him descended many prominent men, including President Elliot of Harvard College. We find that a shoemaker of note, Thomas Beard, resided in Salem in 1629. Also that Thomas Edwards, a name familiar to Beverly people today, resided in the same town. This was in 1649 and in 1652 Jonas Fairbanks was brought before an Essex County court and charged with wearing great boots.

Just before the revolutionary war, Joseph Foster moved to Beverly from Ipswich. He was deacon and also town clerk. He settled on Cabot St., near the way now known as Chestnut St. He was one of those who supplied the Continental Army with shoes during the war. His shop was afterward occupied by Thomas Herrick, who with his sons, Joseph H., now living, Sidney, Emerson, Thomas F. and

SHOES AND SHOEMAKING ILLUSTRATED.

Oliver carried on the business. Geo. F. Herrick residing on the corner of Dane and Hale Streets, the son of Oliver, still continues in the craft. This shop was afterward moved to the corner of Cabot and Myrtle streets and forms, if we mistake not, part of the old house now standing there.

Joseph Foster's son Daniel had a shop on the vacant lot just below the Samuel P. Lovett estate where he manufactured thick, heavy boots, calf skin jackets and petticoat trousers for fishermen. The principal retail trade in shoes was done by the grocers at that time, and Mr. Foster supplied these stores in our own and adjoining towns with men's shoes of various designs.

He shipped also as was customary in those days, shoes to the West Indies and to the southern states, receiving in return all kinds of produce, beans, corn, grain, etc. In connection with shoes, hats, furniture and New England rum formed part of the shipments. These men would occasionally accompany the shipment, both for the sake of the trip and to superintend the sale of the cargo. The following anecdote will illustrate the fearlessness and pluck of these men: During the war of 1812 several of these shoemakers chartered a schooner, loaded her at Essex during the night, ran the blockade successfully, disposed of their cargo at an immense profit securing for themselves a good round sum of money as the result of their venture and the reward of their daring.

Daniel Foster's three sons, James, Seth and Joseph, all worked with him, and later they, under the firm name of Daniel Foster & Son, owned the patent for manufacturing pegged shoes in Essex county. James Foster manufactured shoes in the Gorham Howard house on Bartlett street, also in the original part of the shop where the late Wm. W. Hinkley's house now is.

His son the late Daniel, for many years our worthy assessor, succeeded him in the business until he retired in 1841, to engage in the fishing business.

Seth Foster worked in the business in town until 1874, when he removed to Marblehead and continued the trade there. Many of the older manufacturers of that town learned their trade of him.

In 1829 he removed to Utica, N. Y., and devoted his time to the manufacture of custom shoes in connection with his store there, In 1830 he removed to Newark, N. J., and in the year following to Elizabeth, the same state, where he remained until his death in 1833. It was said of Mr. Foster, that he was the first to introduce pegged shoes into New York State. He was the father of Wm. A. Foster now living at 37 Railroad avenue, whom we all remember was so long in active business on Park St., and who was, we think, the first to introduce steam machinery in connection with the manufacture of shoes in Beverly. Also of Daniel Foster, 2nd, who for many years did a large business on the corner of Railroad avenue and Rantoul St. Joseph Foster, if we are not mistaken, left no children. He worked with his father somewhat, but paid more attention to out of door matters, and experimented largely in the culture of the mulberry with a view to raising silk worms and to the manufacture of silk. For this purpose he set out the orchard of trees near the corner of West Dane and Cabot Streets, and from which Mulberry Street derives its name. His experiments were both interesting and curious, and he was commended by the agricultural department at Washington for his intelligent attention to the subject. But, as it required more capital to successfully develop his experiments than he was able to command, he was never able to meet his expectations in this particular.

SHOES AND SHOEMAKING ILLUSTRATED.

Among those who learned the trade of the elder Daniel were Capt. Daniel Cross, Olphert Tittle and Osman Gage, all seafaring men, the latter the father of Mrs. Charles T. Lovett.

Mr. Tittle carried on an extensive business where Green's Drug Store now is. .

Deacon Nehemiah Roundy had a shop near the northerly corner of the Kittredge estate on Cabot St. At this time it was customary for apprentices to serve seven years and to board with their masters. Some were bound out at a very early age and served until they were 21. One little orphan boy was bound to a shoemaker at the age of 7. When he was 14 he remarked to a companion that he was the happiest boy alive, for he had only 7 years more to serve. The deacon introduced the system of apprentices serving 14 months. At the end of that time they considered their trade learned and received journeymen's wages. He had many apprentices under this system, and some of them have been and are today among our most noted and influential citizens. Out of the many we will mention but one, a name familiar to all Beverly people the late Hon. John I. Baker.

Mr. Roundy built the shop now the Dane house on Cabot Street, having sold the old one to Jeremiah

SHOES AND SHOEMAKING ILLUSTRATED.

Trask, Jr., who removed it across the street. He (Mr. Roundy) manufactured the celebrated Wellington Boot, a very popular and leading style at that time. He shipped shoes to Africa and other foreign countries and also had a very successful home trade in Boston, and for many years made his weekly trip over the road with his one-horse team. He afterward sold the second shop and moved nearer home into the shop now occupied as a dwelling house by Benjamin Holden. Three of his sons, John P., Augustus and George worked with him, the latter doing quite an extensive business even after he had engaged in the lumber trade. Among those who worked in this old shop of Mr. Roundy's, near his dwelling house, was Joseph Woodbury, 2nd, who for many years manufactured shoes on the corner of Railroad Avenue and Hardy street, and who after his death was succeeded by his son Myron, who still continues in the trade. George A. Woodbury, 2nd, another son, was for years located near the corner of Park and Bow streets, and did quite an extensive business there. Joseph Masury is another who worked in this same shop. He afterward did a large and successful business in Cleveland, Ohio, and other Western cities, and is at present we believe, residing at or near the former place. James Hill who was so long our efficient town clerk, and who for many years was so prominent in town affairs, was another of Deacon Roundy's employes. William Goodrich carried on the business in the Luke Goodrich house near the corner of Dane and Cabot streets. His sons Charles, Luke and William, worked with him, the latter being the father of Calvin and Charles W. Goodrich. The house where Calvin now resides was formerly the property of his grandfather. About the year 1819, Capt. Thomas . B. Smith bought the Benjamin Roundy estate adjoining the William Goodrich house. He enlarged and altered the house to its present size and shape, and built here a large factory where he did an extensive business in the manufacture of heavy boots and shoes. This shop was for many years a sort of reform headquarters where anti-slavery, temperance, freemasonry and many other radical measures were discussed, and which found earnest support and many able advocates. His brother, John G. Smith, worked with him. This shop was afterwards moved down on Railroad avenue near the depot, and forms a part of the Railroad House formerly owned by the late

SHOES AND SHOEMAKING ILLUSTRATED.

Jeremiah Murphy, and recently moved to River street.

In 1830, David Lefavour began the manufacture of women's morocco walking shoes in the shop on the Capt. Issachar Foster estate, now owned by Stephen S. Woodbury at the cove. He found a market for

his goods, through a kinsman, in Providence, R. I., and gained for them an excellent reputation. He also took short term apprentices. His business increased until he was obliged to build larger at the cove, and when his son Joseph W., became of age

SHOES AND SHOEMAKING ILLUSTRATED.

BRAY, STANLEY & WEBBER is one of the youngest firms in the city having been organized but a few years. The firm is composed of Clifford B. Bray, who at present represents Ward one in the board of aldermen, Ralph D. Stanley and Louis D. Webber. They are all young men but are men of experience in the business. Mr. Bray was for years general superintendent of the J. A. Wallis factory. He superintends the manufacture. Mr. Stanley has had long experience as a salesman and upon him devolves the duty of selling the product. Mr. Webber is a designer of patterns and a practical cutter, and looks after that end of the business. The specialties of the firm are Misses' and Children's machine sewed, and old ladies' warm goods. They make only for the jobbing trade their goods being shipped to New York, Philadelphia, Chicago, and the North West.

R. E. LARCOM is one of the best known shoe manufacturers in the city having been connected with the industry since the age of 19 years. He was for many years in the shoe finding business, embarking in the manufacture of shoes some eight years ago. He makes a specialty of Misses' and Children's spring heel shoes, and his goods are conceded to be second to none made in the city. Mr. Larcom occupies the large C. H. Cressy factory on Park street. The output is handled entirely by jobbers, and he has attained an enviable reputation among retailers and consumers. The business is under the entire supervision of Mr. Larcom, who is an able and efficient business man and a thorough shoemaker.

and was associated with him, the business increased still more, and he was ultimately obliged to build the large and convenient factory on Rantoul street, where after the father's death, the business was carried on by the son, until his death a short time since. John Lefavour, a brother of David, commenced the manufacture of shoes in 1847. He was, during the early part of his life, a seafaring man, being engaged in the merchant service and bank fishing. For some two years he manufactured goods for the Cuba trade, his shop being on Ober street at the Cove. In 1864 he removed his business to Park street near the depot, and took into partnership his son John H. He coninued in the business until his death in 1872.

Nearly opposite the place where David Lefavour started in business stood the little shop where the name Woodbury Brothers may be said to have originated. In this little shop (which has since been removed and which is now used as a shed upon the premises of the present Woodbury Bros.), Thomas

SHOES AND SHOEMAKING ILLUSTRATED.

Eight years ago SOLON LOVETT started in a small way to manufacture sole leather cut stock. The business under his careful foresight has steadily increased until today he employs twenty-five to thirty workmen making top lifts, soles, counters, taps, etc., which find a ready sale not only in Beverly, and surrounding towns but all over New England. From the little shop near the Boston & Maine depot he moved into larger quarters in the Myron Woodbury factory, until he moved to his present building on Federal street. This building has been enlarged since its occupancy, to meet the constantly increasing business. Mr. Lovett is a man of natural executive ability and is also a practical man whose experience in the details of the business enables him to produce stock which is in demand with the trade. By his own unaided exertion he built up his large trade. Mr. Lovett is also an extensive real estate promoter and has developed successfully several large tracts of land.

SHOES AND SHOEMAKING ILLUSTRATED.

Woodbury, the father of the present firm, with his brothers Elisha, Luther and Stephen, worked at their trade. The present firm also started in this little shop but were soon obliged to build larger there, and have manufactured more goods and employed more help than any other factory in town. Next to the shop of John Lefavour at the Cove was the Boden shop

where Warren, an early apprentice of Deacon Roundy and his brother Porter D., who are now deceased worked at the trade. Opposite this shop was the Galloup shop, where some of the Galloup brothers worked at the trade, of whom Jonas G., alone sur-

SHOES AND SHOEMAKING ILLUSTRATED.

The firm of J. A. WALLIS & CO. is one of the oldest established houses in the city. In one chapter of this book, we find that the firm have succeeded in direct line to the business. This firm was founded in 1867, by Cressy & Wallis. They started in a small way, but were so successful that the present factory corner of Park and Bow streets was erected. The business continued under this name until 1877, when on the death of Mr. Cressy the style of the firm was changed to Wallis, Kilham & Bray. Messrs. J. C. Kilham and S. B. Bray having been taken into the concern a few years previous, and in 1892, Messrs. Kilham & Bray retired, Mr. Wallis continuing alone, until a year or more ago, he took his two sons Arthur C. and Percy into partnership with him, the firm now being J. A. Wallis & Co. They make Dongola button and polish in McKay sewed and Goodyear welts, together with some heavy and warm goods and oxfords. These goods are sent to all sections of the U. S. and to Australia. One specialty is their hand process, machine sewed shoe, which is in great demand throughout the trade.

J. H. SANBORN, Manufacturer of Old Ladies' Machine and Hand Sewed Boots and Shoes and Oxford Ties, in the Norwood Building, Railroad Avenue. Mr. Sanborn is a practical shoe man, engaged in the manufacturer of Children's Shoes from 1887 to 1893, since which time he has been engaged in making the specialties mentioned above. He has a well equipped plant, and manufactures for both the wholesale and retail trade, and his goods which are styled. "Old Ladies' Comfort," "Always Easy," have won for him an enviable reputation, as a Shoe Manufacturer.

vives. Samuel W., a son of Samuel Galloup, and who for many years was connected with David Lefavour & Son, still continues in one branch of the trade on South street, Boston. John O. Standley now deceased and Thomas Hanners, were among the older workers at this shop. Another old shop was that of Phillip Hammond down at Ober's point. Mr. Hammond used to give out shoes to the boys to sew

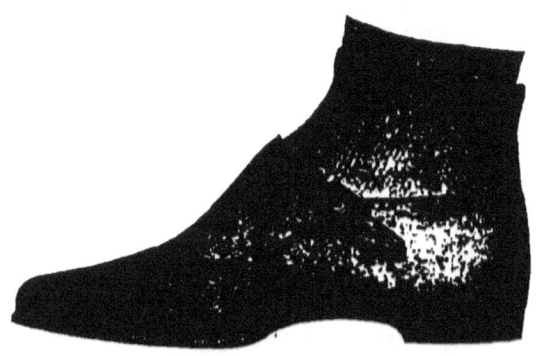

at four cents per pair. Phillip A. Hammond and Daniel W. Hammond, both of whom are at Haverhill, worked here. Another was the shop of John K. Fielder, which stood just below the hose house, and adjoining Nathan Hull's estate. Here worked Benjamin L. Foster, John W. Abbott and many others whose names are familiar ones to-day. This shop, which has since been removed to Lothrop

SHOES AND SHOEMAKING ILLUSTRATED.

Mell. Woodbury

Geo. Millett

There is as good a chance for a young man to start in the shoe business now as there was twenty-five years ago, criers of "hard times" to the contrary notwithstanding, and Beverly is the place to do it in.

A few hustling young men have set an example, now let others follow and keep Beverly in its present place as a leader in the list of shoe cities. Shall not the prosperity which has been given to our city by the push and enterprise of the young men of 30, 40 and 50 years ago be continued through the efforts of the hustling young men of today? Give the young men a chance, capitalists. Don't be conservative. Conservatism has been the ruin of some of our smartest manufacturing cities. Enterprise and business ability are deserving of appreciation and demand encouragement.

The shoe industry is the heart and source of Beverly's prosperity and the foundation upon which it has reared itself. Let us keep the life current throbbing and add to the structure

Levi J. Woodbury   Millett, Woodbury & Co.   Perley G Eldredge

are examples of what can be done here. The members of this firm are George Millett, who personally attends to the stock department, Perley G. Eldredge who superintends the manufacture, Levi J. Woodbury who has charge of the packing and shipping room, and Melville Woodbury who buys the stock and sells the product. They are all energetic, progressive business men, each attending to his own department and all working for their constantly increasing trade.

street, was a sort of a rendezvous for the boys, who used to meet here evenings and learn to play the violin and other instruments, and many a good time has been enjoyed in this place. Israel Foster, the father of Capt. Samuel Foster, had a shop at Chapman's corner and did considerable business there. There were other shoe shops in this neighborhood in which worked Ezra S. Foster, Larkin West and many others. The shop of Ezra Cleaves, on the corner of Dane and Essex streets was another of the older ones in that vicinity, as was also the shop of Hezekiah and George Wallis, near their homestead on the corner of Cabot and Pond streets. George Lampson's shop, which stood on Knowlton street, was of a similar character. Wells Smith, who had a shop on the corner of Cabot and Davis, afterward removed to Dane street, where he did a successful business until he, with many others, took the California fever.

WOODBURY BROS. This name is one of the best known in the city, and the firm has a long and interesting history, and for this reason has the author of this work taken it to illustrate the development of the shoe industry in Beverly. Years ago, four Woodbury Bros. made shoes in the little 14x16 shop at Beverly Cove, shown on page 31. Here Rufus H. Woodbury and H. O. Woodbury the present firm and sons of one of the above mentioned brothers, started, first as workmen afterwards as manufacturers. This was in 1869. The first case of shoes was sold to a Beverly manufacturer, the next two to a firm in Boston who have been customers of the firm ever since. In 1870, the factory shown on page 35, was taken by the firm, and two years later they moved into the third factory shown on page 41, which was destroyed by fire in 1891. They moved to Dover, N. H. but in June, 1893 came back to Beverly and moved into the large and commodious factory shown on page 59. They manufacture Women's, Misse ' and Children's shoes which are sold all over the country.

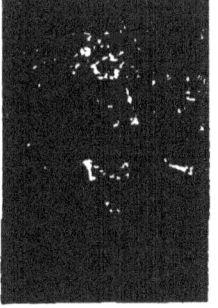

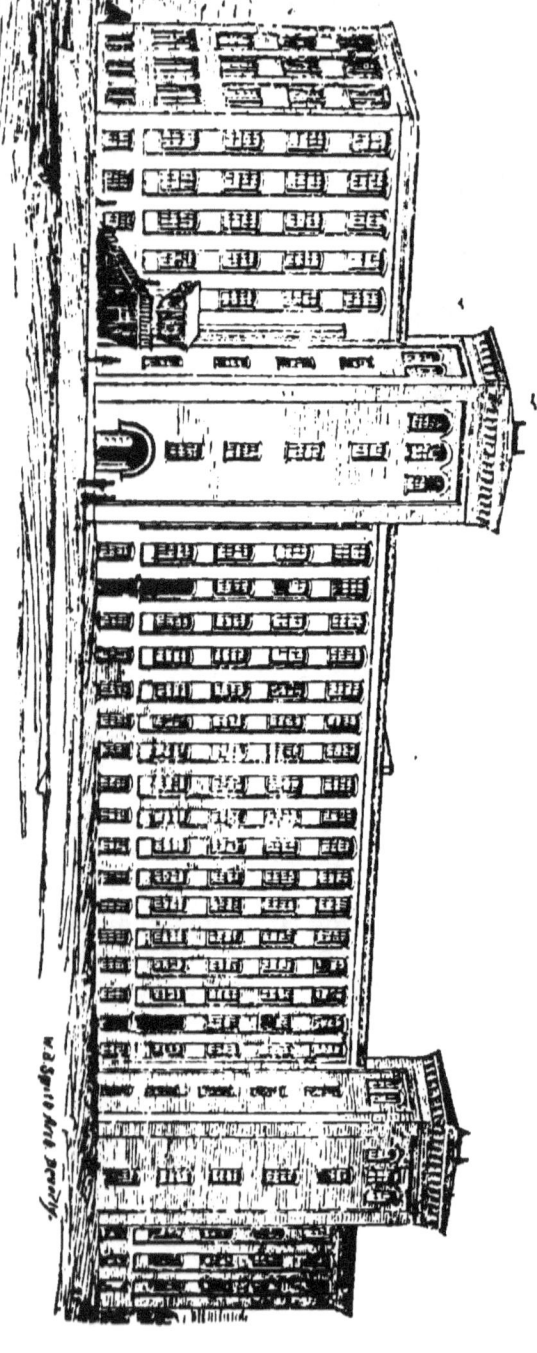

WOODBURY BROS. PRESENT FACTORY.

SHOES AND SHOEMAKING ILLUSTRATED.

JOHN H. HINKLEY & CO. is the name of a live wide awake young firm, who are engaged in business in one of the association factories 61 Rantoul Street. The firm is composed of John H. Hinkley, E. L. Hall, and C. W. Moses, all practical shoemakers. They started in business in the Frank Woodberry building on Park street, May 1st, 1896, and their first year has been a most successful one. They moved a short time since to their present and more convenient quarters. They make a specialty of infant's and children's shoes for the jobbing trade only, and their market is through the South and West.

PERRY & WOOD successors to A. Perry & Co., is the name of the well known shoe firm occupying the factory on the corner of Broadway and Park st. Messrs. Perry & Wood have both had a large experience in the manufacturing of boots and shoes, they having been associated with Mr. Albert Perry a well known and successful shoe manufacturer from 1882 to 1896, when Mr. Albert Perry retired from the business. Their product is sold largely in the New England and Middle States to the jobbing trade. Women's McKay sewed and Goodyear turned medium grade boots and shoes are their specialties, paying particular attention to wide goods.

CHAPTER IV.

Jeremiah Trask, Sr., had a shop on the Joshua Trask estate, near the Gloucester R. R. crossing, where he, with his sons Jeremiah, Nathaniel and Manasseh, did quite a little business. Elbridge, a son of the latter, removed to Danvers later, where he and his sons engaged in the business. Manasseh made shoes to measure near where the Stephen's Baker house now stands. Nathaniel had a shop in the rear of what is now the American Express Co's office. Jeremiah Jr's shop, spoken of in a preceding chapter was near where the present Cabot street store of A. F. Place & Co. now is. Among his apprentices were George S. Millett and the late Seth Norwood, who in connection with his son Francis, built up a large and well known establishment on the corner of Railroad avenue and Rantoul street, and today the Seth Norwood Shoe Co., comprising as it does Francis, William E., Elbridge, Clarence and Charles is one of the best known in the trade.

SHOES AND SHOEMAKING ILLUSTRATED.

CHARLES S. BATCHELDER, manufacturer of ladies' "always easy" shoes for tender feet, Beverly, Mass. This is the way the card of the above firm reads.

Mr. Batchelder begun the shoe business way back in 1869, when he entered the employed of D. Lefavour & Son, Beverly's old time shoe manufacturers. He remained with this firm twenty years, fifteen of which he was foreman of the cutting department and did all the buying for the factory. When this concern went out of business four years ago, Mr. Batchelder went into business for himself. His specialties are old ladies' goods in hand and Goodyear turns, and his product finds a ready market with the leading retailers in New England, the Middle and Western states. Mr. Batchelder is located in the large brick factory on Pleasant street, and his plant is always a busy place.

COLORS NOT NEW.

History repeats itself. So do styles. Colored shoes that we speak of to-day as "new" are old as the hills or something near it. Seventy-two years ago, in 1825, red and green were the popular shades in shoes. In 1850 again the same vagaries of fashion were in force to the extent that footwear matched the costume and reds, browns, and greens were "in it." In olden times colored shoes were always strictly the proper thing—yet here are prating about new styles and modern innovations! We are merely rehashing the fashions of our fathers and grandfathers. Our sons in turn will encounter the same evil.

SHOES AND SHOEMAKING ILLUSTRATED.

Not far from 1830, Mr. Ebenezer Moses who married Miss Ruth Pousland, came here from Malden and set up his business on the corner of Cabot and Essex streets. With him came Wm. D. Crossfield, who married a sister of Mrs. Moses and Mr. Wm. Larabee, brother of Charles A. Larabee. Mr. Moses manufactured mostly run rounds and pumps for ladies and gentlemen. He built a large factory accomodation on the Pousland estate on Chapman street. He was

the first to introduce the division of labor with one to fit the sole, one to sew the shoe and another to finish. He did a large and successful business up to the panic of 1837 and continued for several years after with varied success. His sons, Wm. P., John, James and Charles, worked at the business. Mr. Crossfield, after a few years, went to work at the Connecticut state-prison at Wethersfield, but returned in a short time to Beverly and worked at the trade here.

SHOES AND SHOEMAKING ILLUSTRATED.

To produce handsome stylish and good fitting shoes it is necessary to have patterns that will make these goods. The pattern making business is more than a mere trade, it combines skill and art, besides natural mechanical talent and ability. One of the most successful pattern makers in this vicinity is W. O. CREE. Mr. Cree is also a successful Contract Boot and Shoe stitcher, and all work entrusted to him will be done at short notice and satisfaction guaranteed.

GARDNER & SIMMONS are a hustling young firm doing business at 27 Park street. In the fall of 1895 they bought out the old and established business of George V. Brown, and occupy the entire floor of their building. Their specialty is tips. They use the best patent leather for the work, and their business is constantly on the increase since the inception of the partnership. They have an extensive trade in Beverly and the adjoining cities as the reputation of their goods extends far and wide, the firm receiving orders daily from distant shoe manufacturing centres. Wallace W. Gardner and John H. Simmons comprise the firm, both active, hard working business men who deserve the success which has come to them.

SHOES AND SHOEMAKING ILLUSTRATED.

Mr. Larrabee, although he worked at the trade for some little time, was more or less interested in other matters, being until a short time before his death largely engaged in real estate matters. It is an interesting fact that Samuel Preston of Danvers, who invented

SHOES AND SHOEMAKING ILLUSTRATED.

GEORGE S. BRADSTREET & CO., started in business, manufacturing Heels in October 1895, in the Norwood building basement, they were forced to remove to the J. H. Baker building, at 37 Park street, Nov. 17, 1896, on account of damage to the Norwood building by fire. They manufacture Spring Heels and High Heels from both pieced and whole stock, and have a fine and completely equipped plant and the facilties to carry on their large and constantly increasing business. They supply many of the factories in this city, and some of their product is sold in the surrounding towns.

THOMAS H. LAWRENCE, manufacturer of cut Top Lifts, Counters and Tops, is the successor to Lawrence & Walker. The business was started January 1, 1896, and been successful from the start. Mr. Lawrence is a good judge of stock, and a practical man, having been employed in the sole leather department of Wallis, Kilham & Bray for twelve years previous to his starting in businesss for himself. The product goes to all the shoe towns within a radious of fifty miles from Beverly.

the first pegging machine, was a school teacher in the old brick school house on School street, and after he had removed to Danvers and engaged in the business there, many Beverly persons, including some of his old pupils, worked in his employ. A large part of our people during the preceding century and the early part of the present, were fishermen, who worked at shoemaking during the winter, their work being brought mainly from Lynn and Danvers. Now, instead of our city depending upon these two places for employment, many from these towns are employed in our factories.

Among the old custom shoe-stores were those of Edward Pousland and Samuel Dike, both prominent

SHOES AND SHOEMAKING ILLUSTRATED.

One of the most progressive and successful of the many houses engaged in the manufacture of boys' youths' and liitle gent's shoes in this vicinity, is that of FOWLÈ & DALEY, whose factory and office are located at 17 and 19 Ward street, Salem. Beginning in a very small way on a capital of $300, and making only turned shoes, they have by the excellence of their product built up a trade of very large proportions. The factory occupies fully 12,000 square feet of floor space, and is equipped with the best line of shoe machinery. The product is sold in Boston and New York, and consists of boys', youths and little gents' shoes. One dealer sold 29,000 pairs of one kind of their shoes in a year. This concern cut their own soles and heels, make their taps and use all their own scraps. Every appliance and sanitary improvement has been added for the convenience and safety of the employes. The firm is composed of E. Perley Fowle and Joseph E. Daley, both practical men, who devote their time to supervising the manufacture of their output. Gentlemen, whose integrity and business stability have never been questioned.

citizens, talented and influential; that of the latter is now occupied by Joseph A. Wilson, while that of the former once stood where is now the Grocery Store of George H. Southwick & Son. The Wallis family has long and prominently been identified with the leather craft in Beverly, Nathaniel the first of the name here came from Cornwall, England, and settled at Falmouth, now Portland, Maine, and remained un-

til driven off with the rest of the population by the Indians. He seems first to have come to Manchester, but immediately after to Beverly, settling near the house owned and occupied by the late Augustus Stevens on Cabot Street. Several of his sons were shoemakers of whom Caleb, afterward Deacon Caleb, married in 1687, Sarah a daughter of Nathaniel and Remember Stone, the latter being a daughter of

SOMETHING NEW

THE NAUMKEAG PNEUMATIC CLEANING MACHINE.

This cut shows a Pneumatic Top Arm on a regular Naumkeag Buffing Machine base. It is only a few moments work to put the new top arm on the old machine, and the air foot or cushion automatically filled with air together with the new moulded emery cover is the best thing yet devised for cleaning the soles of boots and shoes. To prove this we refer you to over four hundred manufacturers who have adopted the pneumatic machine during the past year

Naumkeag Buffing Mach. Ass'n.
Beverly. Mass., U. S A.

SHOES AND SHOEMAKING ILLUSTRATED.

Ensign Samuel Corning, who owned all the land from Stephens Hill by Milton street, nearly to Pond street, Corning's Cove near Lawrence's Pottery. Here did Deacon Caleb settle and rear many sons and daughters, many of these sons were shoemakers and their descendants are represented in the craft to this day. The late Deacon Caleb occupied the shop at the corner of Cabot and Wallis streets built by his father Caleb, who carried on the business there, doing mostly custom work. Of the brothers of this latter Caleb who worked in the old one story shoe shop most northerly to the above named shop were Josiah, the father of John E., whose house stands on the site of the old homestead house. Henry the father of Mrs. Edward A. Perry, John a bachelor, who became much interested in horticulture and floriculture and who for many years had charge of the garden and grounds of Col. Israel Thorndike, our present city hall estate, extending from Cabot street corner of Thorndike to Lovett Street and beyond. Several of this family went on fishing voyages, Josiah, we think, more than either. Henry the last survivor of these brothers, stuck to the old shop as long as life and strength permitted, travelling back and forth to

The firm of M. V. BRESNAHAN, is one of the best known in the shoe trade, located in Lynn. The firm consists of M. V. Bresnahan and J. J. Hayes. The concern was established in 1880. They are the manufacturers of the celebrated Bresnahan Automatic Leveller which is unexcelled for rapid and stylish work. They have all the latest models of sole moulding machinery, including the New Duplex Moulder and New Oil Slide Leveller for press work. The reputation of this firm extends throughout the country.

The Boston office is at 122 Summer street.

TOWER, GIDDINGS & CO.

𝔅ankers,

105 Devonshire Street,

BOSTON.

Members of Boston and New York Stock Exchanges.

SHOES AND SHOEMAKING ILLUSTRATED.

"the city" home of his wife, near Beckford street, at one of the many Smith Homesteads, in that vicinity, she being of the race of Hasediah Smith, who was also one of the many driven from their homes on the Eastern shore, near Portland, by the Indians and who sought a home in Beverly. Mr. Smith married the daughter of Edmund Grover whose wife was a daughter of Jacob Barney, who had a very large

farm in what is now Danversport. The Grover homestead was near where Benjamin D. Grant now lives and more or less of the Smith land came from that estate, there were many of the Smith race among the cordwainers, the earliest we have is John Smith, a son of James, born in 1762, who in 1788 bought of his brother James, a portion of the land where was the former home of the city editor, of the Evening Times, nearly opposite Colon street. In the estate

SHOES AND SHOEMAKING ILLUSTRATED.

Consolidated & McKay

Lasting Machine Co.,

Boston, Mass.

 111 Lincoln St.
108 Summer St.
105 Bedford St.

McKay Copeland Lasting Machine Co.
Chase Lasting Machine Co.
Continental Lasting Machine Co.
Consolidated Hand Method Lasting Machine Co.
Boston Lasting Machine Co.

Beverly Building Association
INCORPORATED June 25 1889
BEVERLY, MASS.

of "the first" Deacon Caleb Wallis, in 1714, to shoe maker's seat and settle, are valued at four shillings. Another long cordwainer was Bartholomew Wallis who lived on the corner of Wallis and Cabot streets, in the house purchased some years since by Thomas B. Smith and which was moved to its present location on Cabot street, just above Elliot street. His sons Bartholomew, Andrew, Israel and Levi worked with their father for a time; afterwards for themselves. Bartholomew, Jr., and Andrew W. built the three story house near the corner of Fayette and Cabot streets, the former had a shop in the yard, and the latter made custom shoes to measure, just across the street, near the late John Pickett's house. Israel bought the estate where his son Major Israel now lives. Ebenezer Wallis, who lived on Wallis street (by these names we see that Wallis street was rightly named) made shoes as did his sons Ebenezer, Jr., Joshua and Eleazer. His cousin Ebenezer, whose house was on the site of the Lunt block on the corner of Bow and Cabot streets, had a shop between his house and the Lovett house adjoining, where he worked at his business with his son Ebenezer, Jeremiah, (father of Fred A. Wallis, of the firm of J. V. Porter & Co.)

SHOES AND SHOEMAKING ILLUSTRATED.

William and Joseph, (father of Joseph A. Wallis, of the firm of J. A. Wallis & Sons,) so we see that the business has remained in this family up to the present time and is still in good hands.

A bright and tonguey member of this craft was Jonathan Herrick, whose wife was from the Wallis family. He served during the war of 1812 under Harrison at "Tippecanoe," which appellation he bore ever afterward. His shop, formerly John Hales, was well known as "Tar Bay," and stood on Water street, until it was removed a few years since, when Michael Harrington built his new house on its old

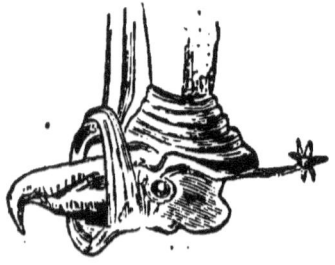

site. Mr. Herrick was the grandfather of Rev. S. Ingersoll Bryant, formerly of this town.

Another character was Harry Ellingwood, who learned his trade of Deacon Roundy, he was lame, and during his youth was a pretty reckless fellow,

SHOES AND SHOEMAKING ILLUSTRATED.

but was converted in later years, and became quite a zealous christian. He emigrated to Kentucky, and was for many years a successful and influential local preacher there.

Lewis Elliot, who married at North Beverly, and who kept a shoe store in Salem, advertised extensively, believing as our wide-awake and energetic dealers do to-day, that a liberal and judicious use of printer's ink pays. Some of his advertisements were attractive for their originality and uniqueness. Many of them are in ryhme. One of his verses read thus:

> "Cheap, cheap, cheap was the cry
> From Buffum's corner to the neck;
> Shoes to buckle shoes to tie,
> Neatly will your feet bedeck."

Another loyal character who served during the war of 1812, was Josiah Foster, known as "Cape Sire." He lived on Essex Street, near the Joshua Trask House. He worked with Jeremiah Trask, Jr., and in some conditions and on some occasions while telling of scenes through which he had passed, would imagine himself on board a man-of-war, and that those associated with him were all Englishmen, and would often "clear the deck" of the whole shops crew.

SHOES AND SHOEMAKING ILLUSTRATED.

A very tall shoemaker known as Jack Ayers, who lived on the estate now owned by Charles H. Patch, near bald hill, had an entry built on to his shop, in order, it was said, to accomodate his legs, and the boys took special delight in twitting him of it, serving to provoke him almost beyond endurance, and this was one of their songs of annoyance:

"It was long tall Jack
Said his whip he would crack,
On the wicked boys back
Who persisted in calling him "Lofty"
But "aloft what's the weather?
They all answered together,
And they would then change his name
to Softy.

Mr. Ayers, was a soldier in the militia, and of such great length of limb that no one else could keep step with his enormous strides, hence he was allowed to

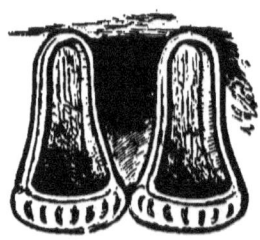

fall out on the march. Had he lived these modern days of pedestrianism, he would no doubt been a champion walker. More than fifty years ago a boy by the

SHOES AND SHOEMAKING ILLUSTRATED.

name of Abner tried to learn the shoemaker's trade at Deacon Roundy's shop where then worked Thomas L. Pickett, a bright and witty character, who one day examining the production of this young struggler said, "Well Abner, you have made something which we can all worship, for it is the likeness of nothing in the heavens above, or the

earth beneath, and the waters under the earth." And the best of it all was this, the Abner took all the credit of the joke to himself and really thought that its brightness off-set any short coming in the shoe line.

One of the early Wallis shoemakers was Daniel, who lived in a square one story house, in the then open field, where is now the junction of Rantoul and Wallis streets. He too was a cordwainer and reared a large family, including several who worked at that trade. In the later years of his life he came under the delusion that he was dead and in constant association with those who had gone before. Hence he was known as "Deadman Daniel," to distinguish him from another Daniel Wallis, a blacksmith, the grandfather of our present Daniel of Federal street, the well known builder. It may be that there was something akin to modern spiritualism in the controlling influences which thus developed themselves in those early days.

CHAPTER V.

It may be of interest to know that the first shoe factory in the United States was located in the neighboring town of Danvers. It was established by Zerubbabel Porter, who waxed prosperous by making heavy brogans for slaves in the south. These were made by hand in the cheapest manner as possible. Following this there were other small shops, which sprang up about the beginning of the century. The uppers, soles and linings were cut by hand and then they were given out to the people of the vicinity to be finished, the women folks doing the stitching and the rest of the work being done by the men who were mostly farmers or fishermen and worked at the trade during their spare time. Hundreds of families added to their scanty income in this way. At this time all the shoes were sewed. One specialty was fisherman's boots, heavy clumsy affairs, which the local shoe makers would make up and take to our wharves, and the neighboring seaport towns for sale. Some time later pegging work was introduced. **Just before the war the uppers began to be stitched**

SHOES AND SHOEMAKING ILLUSTRATED.

on machines, and now everything is done in that way. Perhaps a short description of the process of making the shoes from beginning to end may be of some interest, we will commence at the cutting room. This is the only room in the factory where there is no machinery, and machinery will never be introduced here, for the cutting of the upper demands something more than mere mechanical skill, it needs intelligence and that intelligence is only acquired by long practice and association with leather.

A skin is apt to contain some spot which is too soft or too poor to go into the shoe. That spot is not always seen at once, but it is by the careful and practical touch of the experienced cutter that it is found. These things the successful cutter must know and he must know also just what part of the skin is the best adapted for each part of the shoe upper.

The patterns are hundreds in number and are made of straw board, bound with brass. There are many pieces for each shoe, for a button shoe, the quarters large and small, the vamps, the button fly and the tip, and for the lace shoe the eyelet stay and the tongue. All these separate pieces must have their linings to fit. These uppers are assorted in "case" lots and are sent to the stitching room. Here are the rows of busy

SHOES AND SHOEMAKING ILLUSTRATED.

girls each with a swift running machine before them. Each girl has her special part to perform, one makes the linings or prepares them for the upper, the next one takes and stitches them together at the top, another one puts in the eyelet stay, then it goes to the vamper and then the buttons are sewed on if a button shoe, and the shoe is ready for the lasting machine.

In the mean time the sole has been cut from the heavy side of leather, the counter is fitted in place at the heel, and they are then ready for the pairs of iron hands and jaws that are ready to stretch the upper over the last which has been put in position. While still in the grip of these almost human machines they are tacked securely to the insole. Then the outsole is tacked on and the shoe goes to be sewed, through and through, if it is a McKay sewed shoe and to a shoulder, if it is a turned or a welt shoe. Then the shoe is beat out or levelled, the edges trimmed and the heel put on. This is an interesting process by which fifteen holes are made through the heel and sole, by fifteen awls, then, at a revolution of the machine fifteen nails which have been put in the plate, are driven through and clinched on the iron last. Then the top piece is pressed on to the nails which just stick through the top lift of the heel enough to hold the top on without showing through.

Then the heel is shaped by the heel shaver, then the edges and heels are burnished with blacking or stain with hot irons, the bottoms are smoothed and finished with sandpaper wheels and cleaned with revolving brushes, and the black enamel or stain put on. Then the laces are put in, the sock lining inserted, the shoe carefnlly brushed and cleaned and placed in an individual carton ready for shipment.

A recent editorial in the London " Boot and Shoe Trades Journal" which was reproduced in the "Boot and Shoe Recorder" is of vital interest to the manufacturers of shoes in America. We quote from the editorial as follows.

The predominant characteristic of American boots is that they are stylish and attractive, and it is singular to note that the keenest competition has been in ladies' goods, while no material headway has been made in gents' goods, because attractiveness tells more than anything with regard to women's footwear, whilst in men's goods other considerations have weight. They accommodate themselves readily to the feet. This is the result of two things, the lightness and suppleness of the upper stock, which n no case has all the stretch taken out in lasting, because lasting is slovenly done in America compared with the way it is, or was, done in this country, and again the lasts are designed to give plenty of room without the appearance of extra size. The inner joint is thrown over the sole, a lot of spring put into the sole, and the bottom is, figuratively speaking, as round as an apple.

American shoes are light, they are soft, and as a result they are flexible; lastly, they are cheap, which is a vital consideration. But are they cheaper than British made shoes? It is difficult to make the comparison, for they are so widely different. All our goods contain more material, and if the "timber" were taken out we do not doubt the possibility of a successful competition. In fact many manufacturers assert and have proved their ability to make similar goods at lower rates.

There are points, however, in which American shoes fall far behind the English, and this is why they will be confined to limited sale, and principally to women's work. They do not conform to our ideas as to substance, and when we have exhausted all the praise in favor of the lightness and flexibility of the American goods we are forced to the conclusion that

SHOES AND SHOEMAKING ILLUSTRATED.

British climate and British requirements need a stouter and more substantial foot covering. Cold and rheumatism ever threaten the wearer of knife edge shoes here, and the nature of the passing winter is the best answer to the problem of thin or thick boots.

You say wear rubbers! Yes, these articles are good in their way, but there are people who object to them and will not wear them, and as the secret of business is to make what customers want, and not what one would like them to have, there the question must rest. Now it is a fact, and doubtless many have noticed it, that the moment you begin to put weight and substance into an American boot it instantly begins to lose its attractiveness. Thus it is that the American goods will be confined to a lighter class of boots and shoes. They fill, and will doubtless continue for some time to fill, a certain want, but as our factories are now equipped with fine machinery, and employers and workman are aroused to a proper frame of mind, and determined to cope with any competition, the trade, we repeat, must of necessity be a limited one.

If Americans want to do a trade here, if they want to keep the bit they have got, there is one fact that they have to bear in mind, and that constantly, that is, the importance of delivering bulk orders equal to sample. This, at least, some of them do not do, others may; but it is a sore point with buyers of American footwear, and it is a trouble which will stand in the way of further progress until time and experience prove that sample and bulk agree. If on the other hand, English manufacturers desire to keep the American trade in check, or may be limit it yet further, they too, have some things to observe. They must cultivate a degree of lightness in their goods consistent with solidity and durability, and the first step in that direction lies in giving more attention than they do to the stock they use for uppers. They must also study the question of attractiveness. Most of the prevailing patterns of Amercian goods are old English or variations thereof. Somehow, within the last few years English boots and shoes have been of the plainest and handsomeless design, as if an attempt had been made to imitate old-fashion country bespoke work; but there is not only room, but a demand for more art in British footwear, and a large unconquered field lies before the skillful and artistic shoe designer. Last, but not least, the English manufacturer must limit his variety, for this is the only way he can decrease the cost of production; and decrease it he must and that contiually, or he will find the mechanical shoe maker of America a far more painful thorn in his side. than he is today. Whether it will be necessary to make and sell from stock instead of to order absolutely is a matter which time will have to prove, but there is no mistaking the fact that indications point that way. Machinery seems to demand it, the fitfulness of trade encourages it, and competion may at length render this system of production inevitable.

We have dwelt briefly on the history of footwear, from very early times up to the present day, touching the different kinds made, and various styles worn from one century to another, and so on down to this time. We also have given brief outline of the amount

of work done in this country up to the present time, with interesting and instructive statistics. We also touch briefly upon the early manufacturers and dealers in town, filling the whole in with anecdote and

SHOES AND SHOEMAKING ILLUSTRATED.

story. We have no doubt omitted many persons and shops which we would have been pleased to notice, did space permit. Below is a complete list of the shoe manufacturing establishments in the city, to the present time with their location.

Babb, Williams, Douglas Co., 47 Park Street.
Baker, J. H. & Co., 39 Park Street.
Baker, Louis P. 41 Park Street.
Batchelder, Chas. S. 58 R. R. Ave.
Bay State Boot and Shoe Co. 75 Park Street.
Bray, Stanley & Webber, 1 Park Street.
Burnham, Louis E., Balch Street.
Caldwell, Edw. J., 594 Cabot Street.
Chase, Lewis H., 104 Bridge Street.
Curtis & Lefavour, 1 Park Street.
Dennis, John J. 2nd, 77 Bisson Street.

Frazier, T. E. & Co., 55 Pleasant Street.
Hassett, D. J. & Co., 59 Rantoul Street.
Hinkley, J. H. & Co., rear 61 Rantoul Street.
Larcom, Edward R., 59 Park Street.
Lunt, Hervey, 68 R. R. Ave.
Marsters & Walker, 55 Rantoul Street.
Millett, Woodbury & Co., 61 Rantoul Street.
Murray, Cone & Co., 53 Rantoul Street.
Norwood, Seth Shoe Co., 85 Rantoul Street.
Nugent Bros., 52 R. R. Ave.
Perry & Wood, 59 Broadway.
Porter, Jeremiah L., 58 R. R. Ave.,

SHOES AND SHOEMAKING ILLUSTRATED.

Raymond & Mader, 1 Park Street.

Rogers, S. M. Shoe Co., 37 Park Street.

Sanborn, J. H. & Co., 55 Pleasant Street.

Seavey, F. A. & Co., 59 Rantoul Street.

Thissell, Arthur P., 130 Park Street.

Tuck, Walter E., & Co., 55 Broadway.

Wallis, J. A. & Co. 65 Bow Street.

Warren, A. W. & Co., 64 R. R. Ave

Wilson, John, 63 Federal Street.

Woodberry, Frank, 81 Park Street.

Woodbury Bros., 40 Rantoul Street.

Woodbury, Myron 55 Bow Street.

To any who have contributed in any way in the compilation of this work, the publisher extends thanks, and also to the advertisers, all of whom are reliable and can be heartily recommended to the community.

SHOES AND SHOEMAKING ILLUSTRATED.

How much a man is like old shoes!
For instance, each a sole may lose.
Both have been tanned—both are made tight
By Cobblers—both get left and right.
Both need a mate to be complete,
And both are made to go on feet.
They both need heeling; oft are sold,
And both in time, turn all to mould.
With shoes the last is first; with men
The first shall be last, and when
The shoes wear out they're mended new.
When men wear out, they're men dead, too!
They both are trod upon and both
Will tread on others—nothing loath.
Both have their ties and both incline.
When polished in the world to shine;
And both peg out. And would you choose
To be a man or be his shoes?

ADVERTISEMENTS

GLENWOOD
Ranges and Furnaces
Are The Best.

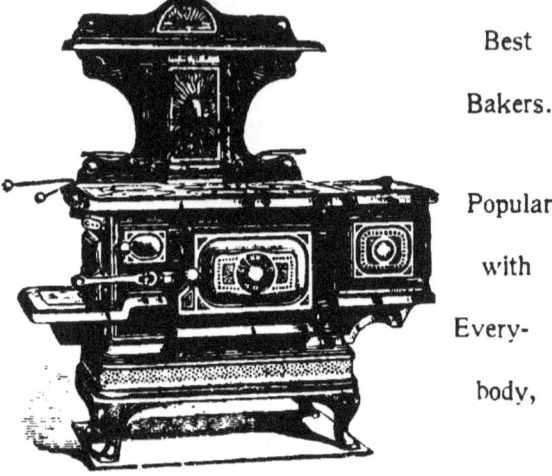

Superior in Construction.

Economical in fuel.

Best Bakers.

Popular with Everybody,

and Low in Price.

We are Headquarters for the Glenwood Ranges, Alaska Refrigerators and Ice Chests. Blue Flame Oil Stoves, Wall Papers, Crockery, Straw and Oil Carpets, and Kitchen Furnishings. Ice Cream Freezers, Hammocks, Window Screens, and all kinds of Piazza Chairs.

A. C. LUNT,
214 Cabot St.,   -   Beverly

ADVERTISEMENTS

No Manufacturer in Beverly

or elsewhere, who is posted in his business, it is safe to assert, in purchasing the various items of materials and labor which enter into the finished product of his factory, could be induced to by any pretext or for any purpose to choose the INFERIOR quality of the several commodities, were the BEST to be offered at the same price; the person making such a proposition to him would be treated as a drivelling idiot.

But when the same manufacturer comes to select the item of INSURANCE which forms the basis of credit for all his operations, how then? Does he make any comparison of the different "GOODS" offered? We think not! But nevertheless there is just as wide a difference in the quality of insurance offered as there is in the quality of stock and materials used, but unlike the stock and materials the Best quality costs no more than the poorest. Therefore, don't be induced to take year after year policies the value of which is all a matter of conjecture with you. Be posted! You pride yourself that you are in every other department of your business. We are in the business to prove the quality of the goods we sell. We ask no more for the 1st class article than you pay for the poor one. Let us talk with you about it! It will be worth your while!

Arthur A. Forness,

Room 3.   *Endicott Bldg, Beverly.*

Representing 14 of the Largest and Strongest Home and Foreign Companies.

ADVERTISEMENTS

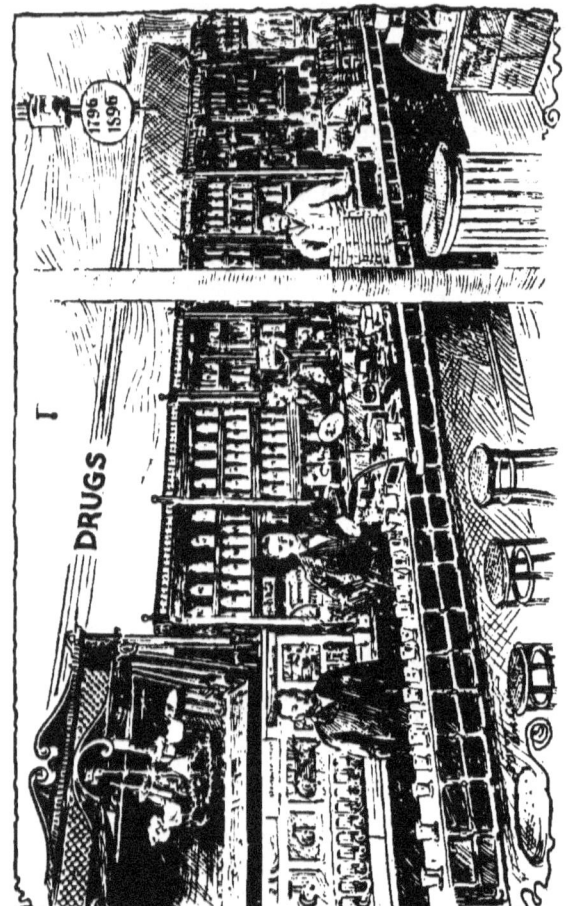

at the old Corner Drug Store.
Established 100 years ago.

Horace Standley,
Prop.

ADVERTISEMENTS

Hinkley's Old Stand.

❦❦❦❦❦❦❦❦

Every RICHMOND is warranted.

In NO respect is it surpassed.

In SOME respect it is unrivalled.

The RICHMOND GRATE keeps fire with least attention.

Its SIMPLICITY commends it.

When in doubt buy a RICHMOND.

❦❦❦❦❦❦❦❦

F. A. HINKLEY & CO.,

91 CABOT ST.

Up-to-date Kitchen Furnishers.

ADVERTISEMENTS

Mrs. A. A. MOORE

Designer and Maker of **Fine Millinery**

Butterick Patterns.

*Agent for Lewando's Dye House.
Headquarters for Dolls.*

No. 105 Cabot Street, Beverly

Girdler's Coal Whaves,

15 Cabot Street and
78 Water Street

Anthracite and Bituminous *COAL.*

HARD AND SOFT WOOD Sawed and Split to order.

ADVERTISEMENTS

Stop Paying Rent! Own your own Home

Beverly Co-Operative Bank

155 Cabot St., Affords the opportunity.
BEVERLY, MASS.

Geo. F. Hinkley no 77 Cabot St. opposite Pleasant St., Beverly Mass. Where you can find the highest grade of Ranges, Furnaces, and tinware Twenty-seven years experince in the Furnace and Stove work in Beverly. If you deal with me, that experience is worth something to you. Lowest cash prices on all goods which are high in standard, and fully warranted. Practical store man, oldest stand in the county. Orders by mail promptly attended. We carry the largest line of Ranges in the city also the best furnace for a low price. Call on us and be convinced. No. 77 Cabot St., Agent for Hot Water Heaters Steam and Hot Air and Hot Water combined. We represent Smith & Anthony goods who are the leading manufacturers in this line of goods, sanitary plumbing

77 CABOT STREET.

ADVERTISEMENTS

Massachusetts Cleansing Co.,
54 Munroe St., Lynn.   R. W. Filene, Manager.

"CLOTHES MAKE THE MAN"

We will call for your Clothes once each week, sponge, clean, press, and repair them (small repairs) and return them to your residence for $1.25 per month, or $12 per year, payable in advance.

IT REALLY COSTS YOU NOTHING,

Because Clothes so well taken care of will average double wear, and look like new all the time. References by permission:

E. A. Maloon, S. B. Bray, A. Whitcomb, C. A. Lamson, J. C. Kilham, Rev. A. B. Coates, Rev. W. A. Bacon, I. W. Foster, J. R. Pope, L. L. Woodbury, C. A. Hurd, E. Giles, Dr. W. H. Swan, Dr. G. A. Stickney, Dr. W. E. Bongartz, Dr. C. W. Haddock, Dr. H. D. Lambert and a hundred others.

P. S. Kindly drop us a postal and our representative will call and explain our system.

E. C. CANN

Contractor and Builder.

Estimates furnished at short notice.

Personal attention given to jobbing.

First-class work guaranteed.

Shop
**124 Rantoul St.,
Beverly**

ADVERTISEMENTS

Marshall & Moulton
EXPRESS COMPANY.

Freight and Express matter forwarded to Boston, New York, Philadelphia, Baltimore and all principal points.

Leave Beverly Office, for Boston, 8.15, 10 and 2 o'clock. Freight at 6.30 o'clock.

Boston Office.—32 and 33 Court square, 105 Arch street, 76 Kingston street. Main office 15 Devonshire street.

VICI KID SHOES for SUMMER WEAR

There is nothing so nice as a good light weight Shoe for warm weather, and Vici Kid Shoes are light, easy and durable. We have them in colors of **CHOCOLATE, GREEN, BROWN, TAN, BLACK.** Our prices are always the lowest.

CENTRAL SHOE STORE.
Commercial Block, BEVERLY, MASS.

H. I. Wilson, Manager.

ADVERTISEMENTS

TOO MUCH, Cannot be said in praise of RAYMONDS SIX PELLETS, for colds. They should be taken on the first indication of a cold and the result is invariably a cure.

Thousands of these Pellets have been used and the demand is constantly increasing. The most effective way to ward off Pneumonia and serious Lung Troubles, is to have a bottle of **RAYMOND'S SIX PELLETS** in the pocket, and use them when needed. They are sold everywhere at 25 cents per Bottle.

Centennial Grove,

ESSEX, MASS.,

The finest PICNIC GROVE and CAMPING GROUND in Massachusetts, magnificent scenery along the shores of Chebacco Lake, an unlimited extent of old primeval pine and spruce forest, interspersed with open glades & smooth drives. Among its many attractions are a Bicycle track, Dance hall, Shooting gallery, Swings, Dining rooms, etc. The safest of Boats are maintained for the use of visitors. The best of facilities for transportation by the Boston & Maine railroad a branch of which runs direct to the grove.

For particulars and terms apply to DAVID LOW, Essex, Mass.

ADVERTISEMENTS

The best ICE-CREAM

The Largest variety of Cake and Pastry in the city.

AT

Payson's

161 Rantoul St., Beverly.

JOHN C. FOWLER, MASON.

Office cor. Pond and Rantoul Streets.

CONTRACTOR

AND

JOBBER.

White-washing Ceilings a specialty.

ADVERTISEMENTS

Lee & Cressy,

←Undertakers

AND FUNERAL DIRECTORS.

Carriages and Hearse Furnished.

All work pertaining to the dead attended to promptly and carefully, day or night.

232 CABOT ST.,   **Beverly**

Telephone No. 757-2

BEVERLY ICE CO.,
- - OFFICE - -

89 PARK STREET, Beverly, - - Mass.

Monthly Rates.

12 Lbs. Daily, per. month $1.50
16   "   "   "   " $1.75
20   "   "   "   " $2.25
30   "   "   "   " $3.25

By weight.

100 Lbs. one Delivery, 25 cents.
 50   "   "   "   15 "
 25   "   "   "   10 "

ADVERTISEMENTS

GEORGE SWAN,

ARCHITECT

BEVERLY, - . MASS.

Bonaventura's

Dealer in

Foreign and Domestic  FRUITS,

French and American Confectionery,
Tobacco, Cigars, etc.

We carry none but the best.

125 Cabot and Cor. Hale and Cabot Sts., Beverly.

ADVERTISEMENTS

GRADUATE OF
Mount Allison Conservatory of Music.
LESSONS GIVEN ON
Piano, Organ and Harmony.

Large experience.

**28 Atlantic Ave.,
BEVERLY.**

Good references.

The best and cheapest **Wood**

For Fire-places and Air-tight Stoves.

✿✿✿✿✿✿✿

KINDLINGS By the Bushel.

J. J HARRIGAN

Foot of Pleasant St

Near Murphy's Stable.

ADVERTISEMENTS

Massachusetts Mutual LIFE INSURANCE CO.

Writes all forms of policies.

Charles L. Dodge,

GENERAL AGENT,

41 Washington Street, - Beverly, Mass.

WM. L. WOOD,
Contract Stitcher of Boots and Shoes,
55 Pleasant Street, Beverly.

BEVERLY LOAN COMPANY,

Money Loaned on Furniture, Pianos, Organs, Horses, Carriages, or any good security. Property to remain in the owners hands.

Mileage Books to let.

Boston Tickets for sale.

55 Pleasant Street, Beverly.
WM. L. WOOD, Manager.

ADVERTISEMENTS

UNION STABLES,
West Dane Street, Beverly, Mass.
W. M. STEVENS, Prop.

When you ride take your ease.

Rubber Tires for comfort

First-class Boarding and Livery Stable. Fine Horses and Modern Equipages.

Cosy Homes.

Do you contemplate building or purchasing Real Estate. If so, do not fail to investigate this very desirable property.

On Mason Street, North Beverly, finely built cottages of 6, 7 and 8 rooms, with all modern conveniences, for sale for cash or easy payments. This property is located on the right of Cabot Street, north of Gloucester Crossing, having all the advantages of fine view and pure air. Electric cars pass the head of the street every 15 minutes. For terms apply to

L. K. BARKER, Wenham Depot,
or S. H. STONE'S REAL ESTATE AGENCY.

ADVERTISEMENTS

BEVERLY MACHINE WORKS,

Contractors,
  General Machinists,
    Millwrights.
      Machine Jobbers and
        Repairers,
          Nickel Platers,
            Brass Finishers and Polishers.

Rear of Association Factory No. 4,

61 Rantoul Street,   Beverly, Mass.

Boston Office: 13 Doane St., Room 8.

John S. Baker, Manager.   William E. Bailey, Superintendent.

L. C. CURRIE,

Carpenter, - Contractor - and - Builder.

26 West Dane Street, - Beverly, Mass.

Plans, Specifications
and Estimates
furnished free.

Jobbing and Repair-
ing promptly done.

ADVERTISEMENTS

W. K. Woodbury,
Teacher of Piano,
6 Dane St., Beverly.

Special attention to beginners

Joseph Pickett — Dealer in
Cigars, Tobacco,

and all kinds of Smokers' Articles,

236 Cabot Street, Beverly

Opposite Car Station.

Agent for Beverly Custom Laundry.

ADVERTISEMENTS

BEVERLY SAVINGS BANK,

177 Cabot Street cor. Thorndike St.
BEVERLY, MASS.

Open Daily from 8.30 a. m. to 1.30 p. m.

Robert R. Endicott, Pres.   Chas. H. Kilham, Treas.

Albert S. Hoogs, Teller.

Committee on investments,

Robert R. Endicott, Augustus N. Clark, Samuel J. Foster, George Butman.

Deposits begin to draw interest on the fourth Wednesdays of January, April, July and October, and may be withdrawn at any time without previous notice.

Dividends payable on the fourth Wednesdays of April and October in each year, and placed on interest immediately if not withdrawn.

No. of Depositors	Amount of Deposits
6,000	$2,100,000

Beverly, March 1, 1897.

Ira. A. Smith,   Walter L. Dixon.

SMITH & DIXON,
◁ Machinists, ▷

Shoe Machinery built and repaired. Particular attention given Experimental Work. Duplicate Parts for Reece Button Hole, and other Standard Machines always on hand. Pulleys, Hangers, and Shafting, furnished at short notice; also estimates for placing the same.

COR. PARK & PLEASANT STREETS.
━━━BEVERLY, MASS.━━━

ADVERTISEMENTS

Beverly National Bank,

CAPITAL, $200,000.00

ALBERT PERRY, President.

ALLEN H. BENNETT, Cashier

Safe Deposit Boxes to rent, in fire and burglar proof vaults.

Bank Hours: 8.30 A.M. to 2 P.M.

BEVERLY BURIAL VAULT CO.,

T. P. OBER, MANAGER.

Residence Odell Ave., near Cabot.

Manufacturers of

Artificial Stone, Burial Vaults, or Coffin Receptacles.

☞ Orders received by telephone at the drug store of G. C. & J. L. Berry, 259 Cabot Street, Beverly will receive prompt attention.

ADVERTISEMENTS

Andrew M. Ober

Successor to Philip E. Ober,

PATENTEE AND MANUFACTURER OF

PATENT CEMENT

Sarcophagus or Burial Vaults.

Also Cement Water Gates & Hydrant Boxes

Mason Work promptly attended to.

DRAIN PIPE Furnished and Layed.

17 Union St., Beverly, Mass.

THE MURPHY

Livery, Hack and Boarding *STABLE,*

Pleasant St., near Depot Sq., Beverly, Mass.

FIRST-CLASS COACHES

Furnished for Funerals, Weddings and Receptions.

Carriages at Depot to meet all trains. First-Class Horses and Latest Style Carriages To Let at Reasonable Prices.

Calls attended to Day or Night. Barges and Large Carriages Furnished for Parties.

J. F. DESMOND, Prop.

Telephone 723-2.

ADVERTISEMENTS

Fire, Life, Accident, Plate-Glass, Liability, in fact all kinds of

INSURANCE

Written in Largest and Best
STOCK AND MUTUAL COMPANIES
At Tariff Rates.

Dividends of 70 per cent. paid on 5 year policies.

Real Estate Brokers.

Issachar Lefavour & Son,

16 Washington St., Cor. Brown, Beverly, Mass.

Justice of the Peace.   Mortgages Negotiated.

Dress Cutting

By the
TAYLOR SYSTEM
Taught by

Mrs. C. E. Arnold.

DRESS - AND - CLOAK - MAKING.

Seamless Work a Specialty.

2 Milton Street, Corner Cabot Street,

. . . . *Beverly, Mass.*

ADVERTISEMENTS

The Beverly Bowling Alleys,
Corner Rantoul and Bow Streets.

The finest Bowling Alleys in the county. There are seven in all, fitted in elegant style with a new and brilliant system of lights. Prizes offered every week for highest scores.

Come down and roll, when time hangs heavy on your hands, at the Myron Woodbury building.

KEHEW & ODELL,

34 Railroad Ave.   Printers.

This book is a sample of our work.

Salem Office 228 Essex Street.

ADVERTISEMENTS

Samuel A. Gentlee,

FUNERAL DIRECTOR AND EMBALMER.

291 Cabot Street, Beverly.

✿✿✿✿✿✿

Calls answered day or night.

Night calls, 18 Butman Street.

Telephone, 702-2.

Frank E. Ludden,

MILK DEALER

Drop me a postal and I will call.

36 Dodge Street,   Beverly, Mass.

ADVERTISEMENTS
A BEVERLY MAN.

New England's most Noted Healer, challenges the world to exceed his cures. Without the aid of medicine, he cures cases pronounced incurable by the best physicians. No matter if your case has been given up as incurable, go and see him.

Dr. Dennis possesses a power which can not be explained, but its effect upon diseases can not be denied. It is far superior to medicine.

Some of his most marvellous cures have been made in his native city.

Female Diseases a specialty. Office 81 Washington St., Salem, Room 5. Residence Prospect St., Beverly. Hours at Office, from 9 to 4 Wednesday and Saturday.

Clark's Opera House,

TO LET FOR PARTIES.

TERMS REASONABLE.

Accomodations Excellent.

ADVERTISEMENTS

Mrs. M. E. Wallis,

Regular and Transient Boarders.

First-Class Table Board.

Dinners 25 cts.

Table Board, $3.50.

No. 11 Railroad Avenue.

V. L. Rankin, Contractor and Builder.

Jobbing in all its branches.   Estimates Furnished on application.

Shop and Residence,

18 Highland Ave.,   Beverly, Mass.

ADVERTISEMENTS

Established in 1844. Telephone Connections.

The Pickett Coal Co.,
(Successor to John Pickett)
Dealers In

Coal, Wood, Cement, Lime, Sand and Hair.

Offices, 15 Water Street, and
164 Cabot cor. Milton Sts.

Order Box at H. P. Woodbury's, at Cove.

TERMS, CASH.

Burton Avenue leads from Essex to Bisson streets, and is one of the finest Avenues in the City, G. E. & B. electrics pass close by and it is about 6 minutes walk to City Hall, and a few minutes to the Beach, where there is fine Boating and a short row to the Willows. This Avenue is considered the healthiest part of the City, five Cottages already built and sold to good parties, two more being finished and will be For Sale; the Cottages are well built and have modern conviniences and have six and seven rooms and dry cellars. Price reasonable and very easy terms. P. S. It is a fact that these Lots are the nearest to the City Hall, that can be purchased for a reasonable price. Can refer to those I have built.

J. H. MORSE,
71 Essex St.,   Beverly, Mass.

ADVERTISEMENTS

CASH PAID FOR FAT CATTLE,
VEAL CALVES AND FAT HOGS.

New Milch Gows on hand for sale.

Particular attention paid to the
Cleaning Out of Vaults, Cesspools, Etc.,
By the ODORLESS EXCAVATOR PROCESS.

E. B. ROWELL.

☞ Orders may be left at S. A. Gentlee's, 291 Cab- Street, or Box 1322, Beverly, Mass.

For the House, Stable, Poultry House and Kennel,

Cabot's Sulpho-Napthol
Liquid Cleanliness

For sale by

Whitcomb=Carter Co.

ADVERTISEMENTS

He don't know much about shoe-making, but if you want to talk about

FISH

he can tell you that his market is the cheapest place in Beverly.

CARL E. KLINK, Fine Baker & Confectioner.

Delicious Cream Bread and rolls fresh every afternoon.

Wedding, Birthday, and fancy ornamented cake a specialty.

Ice Cream, Sherbet and Frozen Pudding delivered to all parts of the city and vicinity.

143 CABOT STREET, - **BEVERLY, MASS.**

www.ingramcontent.com/pod-product-compliance
Lightning Source LLC
Chambersburg PA
CBHW020125170426
43199CB00009B/645